GENERAL

1. Where there is a pavement or footpath, use it. Where possible, avoid walking next to the kerb with your back to the traffic. If you have to step into the road, watch out for traffic.

2. Where there is no pavement or footpath, walk on the right-hand side of the road so that you can see oncoming traffic. Keep close to the side of the road. Take care at sharp right-hand bends; it may be safer to cross the road well before you reach one so that oncoming traffic has a better chance of seeing you. After the bend cross back to face the oncoming traffic. Walk in single file if possible, especially on narrow roads or in poor light.

Be seen in the dark – wear something reflective.

3. Wear or carry something that will help you to be seen. Light-coloured, bright or fluorescent items will help in poor visibility. At night use reflective materials (eg reflective armbands and sashes) which can be seen in headlights up to three times as far away as non-reflective materials.

4. Do not let young children out alone on the pavement or road (see Rule 7). When taking children out, walk between them and the traffic and hold their hands firmly. Strap very young children in push-chairs or use reins.

5. A group of people involved in an organised march on the road should keep to the left. There should be look-outs in front and at the back wearing fluorescent clothes in daylight and reflective clothes in the dark. At night, the look-out in front should carry a white light and the one at the back a bright red light which is visible from behind. People on the outside of large groups should also carry lights and wear reflective clothing.

6. You **MUST NOT** walk on motorways or their slip roads except in an emergency (see Rule 183).

CROSSING THE ROAD

The Green Cross Code
7. The Green Cross Code gives advice on crossing the road. It is for all pedestrians. Children should be taught it and should not be allowed out alone until they can understand and use it properly. The age when they can do this is different for each child. Many children under ten cannot judge how fast vehicles are going or how far away they are. Children learn by example, so parents should always use the Code in full when out with children. Parents are responsible for deciding at what age their children can use it safely by themselves.

CONTENTS

Page

Introduction   Inside front cover

Pedestrians

GENERAL	3
CROSSING THE ROAD	4
EMERGENCY VEHICLES	9
GETTING ON OR OFF A BUS	9
RAILWAYS AND TRAMWAYS	9

Drivers, motorcyclists and cyclists

GENERAL	10
DRIVING YOUR VEHICLE	13
LINES AND LANES ALONG THE ROAD	20
OVERTAKING	23
ROAD JUNCTIONS	25
ROUNDABOUTS	29
REVERSING	31
VEHICLE LIGHTS	32
WAITING AND PARKING	33
ROAD WORKS	35
BREAKDOWNS AND ACCIDENTS	36

Motorways

GENERAL	37
JOINING THE MOTORWAY	38
ON THE MOTORWAY	38
LEAVING THE MOTORWAY	43

Extra rules for cyclists

CHOOSING AND MAINTAINING YOUR CYCLE	43
SAFETY EQUIPMENT AND CLOTHING	44
CYCLING	45

Animals

GENERAL	47
HORSE RIDERS	48

Railway level crossings

GENERAL	49

Tramways

GENERAL	51
PEDESTRIANS	52

Speed limits   53

Page

Light signals controlling traffic

TRAFFIC LIGHT SIGNALS   54
FLASHING RED LIGHTS   54
MOTORWAY SIGNALS   54
LANE CONTROL SIGNALS   54

Signals by authorised persons

STOP   55
BECKONING TRAFFIC ON   55

Signals to other road users

DIRECTION INDICATOR SIGNALS   56
BRAKE LIGHT SIGNALS   56
ARM SIGNALS   57
ARM SIGNALS TO PERSONS CONTROLLING TRAFFIC   57

Traffic signs

SIGNS GIVING ORDERS   58
WARNING SIGNS   59
DIRECTION SIGNS   61
INFORMATION SIGNS   62

Road markings

ACROSS THE CARRIAGEWAY   63
ALONG THE CARRIAGEWAY   63
ALONG THE EDGE OF THE CARRIAGEWAY   64
ON THE KERB OR AT THE EDGE OF
    THE CARRIAGEWAY   64
ZEBRA CONTROLLED AREAS   65
OTHER ROAD MARKINGS   65

Vehicle markings

HEAVY GOODS VEHICLE REAR MARKINGS   66
HAZARD WARNING PLATES   66
PROJECTION MARKERS   66

The road user and the law

ROAD TRAFFIC LAW   67
PENALTIES   73

Vehicle security   75

First aid on the road   75

Shortest stopping distances   back cover

Note. In the following Rules the words **MUST/ MUST NOT** refer to requirements of the law.

a First find a safe place to cross, then stop.

It is safer to cross at subways, footbridges, islands, Zebra, Pelican and Puffin crossings, traffic lights or where there is a police officer, school crossing patrol or traffic warden. Otherwise choose a place where you can see clearly in all directions. Try to avoid crossing between parked cars (see Rule 23). Move to a space where drivers can see you clearly.

b Stand on the pavement near the kerb.

Stop just before you get to the kerb – where you can see if anything is coming, but where you will not be too close to the traffic. If there is no pavement, stand back from the edge of the road but make sure you can still see approaching traffic.

c Look all around for traffic and listen.

Traffic could come from any direction, so look along every road. Listen also because you can sometimes hear traffic before you see it.

d If traffic is coming, let it pass. Look all around again.

If there is any traffic near, let it go past. Then look around again. Listen to make sure no other traffic is coming.

e When there is no traffic near, walk straight across the road.

When there is no traffic near, it is safe to cross. Remember, even if traffic is a long way off, it may be approaching very quickly.

When it is safe, walk straight across the road – do not run.

f Keep looking and listening for traffic while you cross.

When you have started to cross, keep looking and listening in case there is any traffic you did not see – or in case other traffic suddenly appears.

Crossing where there is a central island in the road

8.   Use the Green Cross Code to cross to the island. Stop there and use the Code again to cross the second half of the road.

Crossing at a junction

9.   When you cross the road at a junction look out for traffic coming round the corner, especially from behind you.

Crossing at a Zebra crossing

10.   If there is a Zebra crossing nearby, use it. Do not cross at the side of a crossing on the zig-zag lines – it is very dangerous.

11.   Give traffic plenty of time to see you and to stop before you start to cross. Vehicles need more time to stop when rain or ice have made the road slippery. If necessary put one foot on the crossing; until you have stepped on to a Zebra crossing, the traffic does not have to stop. But do not cross until the traffic has stopped. Do not push a wheelchair or pram on to the crossing until the traffic has stopped.

12.   When the traffic has stopped, walk straight across but keep looking both ways and listening in case a driver or rider has not seen you and attempts to overtake a vehicle that has stopped.

13.   If there is an island in the middle of a crossing, wait on the island and follow Rules 11 and 12 before you cross the second half of the road – it is a separate crossing.

Crossing at a Pelican crossing

14.   If there is a Pelican crossing nearby, use it. Do not cross at the side of a crossing on the zig-zag lines – it is very dangerous. At this type of crossing the traffic lights instruct the traffic when to stop and pedestrians when to cross. When the red figure shows, do not cross. Press the button on the box and wait. When the lights change to show a steady green figure check that the traffic has stopped and then cross with care. (At some Pelicans there is also a bleeping sound or voice to tell blind or partially sighted people when the steady green figure is showing.) After a while, the green figure will begin to flash. This means that you should not start to cross. But if you have already started you will have time to finish crossing safely.

15. A 'staggered' crossing (see illustration) should be treated as two separate crossings. On reaching the central island you must press the button again to obtain a steady green figure.

Treat staggered crossings as two separate crossings.

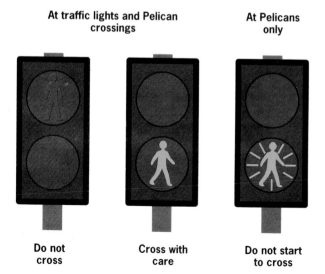

Crossing at a Puffin crossing

16.   Puffin crossings are similar to Pelican crossings except that the pedestrian signals are on your side of the road. After pressing the button, you should wait where indicated for the green figure to show. Infra-red detectors will vary the length of time of the red light for drivers to ensure that pedestrians have enough time to cross safely.

Crossing at traffic lights

17.   Some traffic lights have pedestrian signals similar to those at Pelican crossings. The green figure does not flash but there will be enough time to finish crossing after it goes out. If there are no pedestrian signals, watch carefully and do not cross until the traffic lights are red and the traffic has stopped. Even then, look out for traffic turning the corner. Remember that traffic lights may let traffic move in some lanes while other lanes are stopped.

Crossings controlled by police, traffic wardens or school crossing patrols

18.   Where a police officer, traffic warden or school crossing patrol is controlling the traffic, do not cross the road until they signal you to do so. Always cross in front of them.

Guard rails

19.   Guard rails are there for your safety. Cross the road only at the gaps provided for pedestrians. Do not climb over the guard rails or walk between them and the road.

Tactile paving

20.   Some pedestrian crossing points have textured paving to let blind or partially sighted people know where to stand while waiting to cross the road.

Crossing one-way streets

21.   Use the Green Cross Code. Check which way the traffic is moving. Do not cross until it is safe to do so without stopping. In some one-way streets, bus lanes operate in the opposite direction to the rest of the traffic.

Crossing bus and cycle lanes

22.   Use the Green Cross Code. Vehicles in bus lanes may be going faster than traffic in other lanes. Watch out for cyclists who may be riding in bus or cycle lanes.

Parked vehicles

23.   If you have to cross between parked vehicles, use the outside edge of the vehicles as if it were the kerb. Stop there and make sure you can see all around and that the traffic can see you. Then carry on using the Green Cross Code. Do not stand in front of or behind any vehicle that has its engine running.

Crossing the road at night

24.   Use the Green Cross Code. If there is no pedestrian crossing or central island nearby, cross near a street light so that traffic can see you more easily. It is harder for others to see you at night so wear something reflective.

EMERGENCY VEHICLES

25.   If you see or hear ambulances, fire engines, police or other emergency vehicles with their blue lights flashing or their sirens sounding, **KEEP OFF THE ROAD**.

GETTING ON OR OFF A BUS

26.   Only get on or off a bus when it has stopped to allow you to do so. Never cross the road directly behind or in front of a bus. Wait until it has moved off and you can see the road clearly in both directions.

RAILWAYS AND TRAMWAYS

27.   Take extra care at railway level crossings and near tramways (see Rules 225–234 and 241–242).

DRIVERS, MOTORCYCLISTS AND CYCLISTS

(More detailed guidance is given in The Driving Standards Agency's publications *The Driving Manual* and *The Motorcycling Manual*.)

GENERAL

Vehicle condition

28. You **MUST** ensure your vehicle is roadworthy. Take special care of lights, brakes, steering, tyres (including spare), exhaust system, seat belts, demisters, windscreen wipers and washers. Keep windscreens, windows, lights, indicators, reflectors, mirrors and number plates clean and clear. Ensure your seat, seat belt, head restraint and mirrors are adjusted correctly before you drive.

Loads

29. Any loads carried or towed **MUST** be secure and **MUST NOT** stick out dangerously. You **MUST NOT** overload your vehicle or trailer.

Motorcycles

30. The rider and pillion passenger on a motorcycle, scooter or moped **MUST** wear an approved safety helmet which **MUST** be fastened securely. It is also advisable to wear eye protectors, and strong boots, gloves and clothes that will help protect you if you fall off. Pillion passengers **MUST** sit astride the machine on a proper seat and keep both feet on the footrests. To help you to be seen, wear something light-coloured or bright. Fluorescent material helps in the daylight, as do dipped headlights on larger machines. Reflective material helps in the dark.

Tiredness or illness

31. If you feel tired or ill, **DO NOT DRIVE**.

32. Driving can make you feel sleepy. To help avoid this, make sure there is a supply of fresh air into your vehicle. If you feel tired while driving, find a safe place to stop and rest.

33. You **MUST NOT** drive under the influence of drugs or medicines. When taking prescribed medicines, ask your doctor if it is safe to drive. When taking other medicines, ask the pharmacist.

Vision
34. You **MUST** be able to read a vehicle number plate from a distance of 20.5 metres (67 ft) which is about five car lengths. If you need glasses (or contact lenses) to do this you **MUST** wear them when driving.

35. At night or in poor visibility, do not use tinted glasses, lenses or visors. Do not use spray-on or other tinting materials for windows and windscreens.

Learners
36. Learner drivers in a car **MUST** be supervised by someone at least 21 years old who has held a full British licence for that type of car (automatic or manual) for at least three years and still holds one.

37. If you are learning to ride a motorcycle, scooter or moped you **MUST** take basic training with an approved training body before riding on the road, unless exempt. You **MUST NOT** carry a pillion passenger, pull a trailer or ride a solo motorcycle with an engine capacity in excess of 125cc.

38. All vehicles under the control of a learner **MUST** display L-plates, which should be removed or covered at all other times (except on driving school vehicles).

Alcohol and the motorist
39. **Do not drink and drive.** Drinking alcohol seriously affects your driving. It reduces your co-ordination, slows down your reactions, affects your judgement of speed, distance and risk, and gives you a false sense of confidence. Your driving may be badly affected even if you are below the legal limit (see page 68).

Remember: you may still be unfit to drive in the evening after drinking at lunchtime or in the morning after drinking the previous evening.

Seat belts

40. Wearing seat belts saves lives and reduces the risk of serious injury in an accident. You **MUST** wear a seat belt if one is available, unless you are exempt.

The following table summarises the main legal requirements for wearing seat belts.

	FRONT SEAT	REAR SEAT	WHOSE RESPONSIBILITY
DRIVER	Must be worn if fitted	—	Driver
CHILD UNDER 3 YEARS OF AGE	Appropriate child restraint must be worn	Appropriate child restraint must be worn if available	Driver
CHILD AGED 3 to 11 and under 1.5 metres (about 5 feet) in height	Appropriate child restraint must be worn if available. If not, an adult seat belt must be worn	Appropriate child restraint must be worn if available. If not, an adult seat belt must be worn if available	Driver
CHILD AGED 12 or 13 or younger child 1.5 metres or more in height	Adult seat belt must be worn if available	Adult seat belt must be worn if available	Driver
ADULT PASSENGERS	Must be worn if available	Must be worn if available	Passenger

41. An appropriate child restraint is a baby carrier, child seat, harness or booster seat appropriate to the child's weight.

Children in cars

42. Do not let children sit behind the rear seats in an estate car or hatchback. Make sure that child safety door locks, where fitted, are used when children are in the car. Keep children under control in the car.

Car telephones and microphones

43.   You **MUST** exercise proper control of your vehicle at all times. Do not use a hand-held telephone or microphone while you are driving. Find a safe place to stop first. Do not speak into a hands-free microphone if it will take your mind off the road. You **MUST NOT** stop on the hard shoulder of a motorway to answer or make a call, except in an emergency.

Traffic light signals and traffic signs

44.   You **MUST** obey all traffic light signals (see page 54) and traffic signs giving orders (see pages 58 and 59). Make sure you also know and act on all other traffic signs and road markings (see pages 59 to 65).

Signals

45.   Give signals to help and warn other road users, including pedestrians (see pages 56 and 57). Give them clearly and in plenty of time. Make sure your indicators are cancelled after use.

46.   Watch out for signals given by other road users and take appropriate action.

47.   You **MUST** obey signals by police officers and traffic wardens (see page 55) and signs used by school crossing patrols.

DRIVING YOUR VEHICLE

Moving off

48.   Use your mirrors before you move off. Signal if necessary before moving out. Look round as well for a final check. Only move off when it is safe to do so.

Driving along

49.   Keep to the left, except where road signs or markings indicate otherwise or when you want to overtake, turn right or pass parked vehicles or pedestrians in the road. Let others overtake you if they want to.

50.   You **MUST NOT** drive on a pavement or footpath except for access to property.

51.   Use your mirrors frequently so you always know what is behind and to each side of you. Use them well before you carry out a manoeuvre or change speed; then give the correct signal if you need to. Motorcyclists should always look behind before manoeuvring.

Remember: mirrors–signal–manoeuvre

52. Watch out for cycles and motorcycles. Two-wheelers are far harder to spot than larger vehicles – but their riders have the same rights as other road users and are particularly vulnerable. Give riders plenty of room, especially if you are driving a long vehicle or towing a trailer.

53. Do not hold up a long queue of traffic. If you are driving a large or slow-moving vehicle and the road is narrow or winding, or there is a lot of traffic coming towards you, pull in where you can do so safely so that other vehicles can overtake.

Speed limits
54. You **MUST NOT** exceed the maximum speed limits for the road and for your vehicle (see the table on page 53). Street lights usually indicate a 30 mph speed limit unless signs show other limits.

55. Drive slowly in residential areas. In some roads there are features such as road humps and narrowings intended to slow you down. A 20 mph maximum speed limit may also be in force.

56. A speed limit does not mean it is safe to drive at that speed. Drive according to the conditions. Slow down if the road is wet or icy and in fog. Drive more slowly at night when it is harder to see pedestrians and cyclists.

Stopping distances
57. Drive at a speed that will allow you to stop well within the distance you can see to be clear. Leave enough space between you and the vehicle in front so that you can pull up safely if it suddenly slows down or stops. The safe rule is never to get closer than the overall stopping distances shown opposite. But in good conditions on roads carrying fast traffic, a two second time gap may be sufficient. The gap should be at least doubled on wet roads and increased further on icy roads. Large

Use stationary objects (eg lamp-posts) to help you keep a two second gap.

vehicles and motorcycles need more time to stop than cars. Drop back if someone overtakes and pulls into the gap in front of you.

Shortest stopping distances – in metres and feet				
mph	Thinking distance	Braking distance	Overall stopping distance	On a dry road, a good car with good brakes and tyres and an alert driver will stop in the distances shown. Remember these are shortest stopping distances. Stopping distances increase greatly with wet and slippery roads, poor brakes and tyres, and tired drivers.
20	6 20	6 20	12 40	
30	9 30˙	14 45	23 75	
40	12 40	24 80	36 120	
50	15 50	38 125	53 175	
60	18 60	55 180	73 240	
70	21 70	75 245	96 315	
(See diagram on back cover)				

Fog code
58.   Before driving in fog, consider if your journey is essential. If it is, allow extra time. Make sure your windscreen, windows and lights are clean and that all your lights (including brake lights) are working.

When driving in fog:

- See and be seen. If you cannot see clearly use dipped headlights. Use front or rear fog lights if visibility is seriously reduced (see Rule 133) but switch them off when visibility improves. Use your windscreen wipers and demisters.
- Check your mirrors and slow down. Keep a safe distance behind the vehicle in front. You should always be able to pull up within the distance you can see clearly.

- Do not hang on to the tail lights of the vehicle in front; it gives a false sense of security. In thick fog, if you can see the vehicle in front you are probably too close unless you are travelling very slowly.
- Be aware of your speed; you may be going much faster than you think. Do not accelerate to get away from a vehicle which is too close behind you. When you slow down, use your brakes so that your brake lights warn drivers behind you.
- When the word 'Fog' is shown on a roadside signal but the road appears to be clear, be prepared for a bank of fog or drifting smoke ahead. Fog can drift rapidly and is often patchy. Even if it seems to be clearing, you can suddenly find yourself back in thick fog.

Winter driving

59.   Prepare your vehicle for winter. Ensure that the battery is well maintained and that there are appropriate anti-freeze agents in the radiator and windscreen washer bottle.

60.   In freezing or near freezing conditions, drive with great care even if the roads have been gritted. Roads may be slippery and surface conditions can change abruptly. Take care when overtaking gritting vehicles, particularly if you are riding a motorcycle.

61.   Do not drive in snow unless your journey is essential. If it is, drive slowly but keep in as high a gear as possible to help avoid wheel spin. Avoid harsh acceleration, steering and braking. You **MUST** use headlights when visibility is seriously reduced by falling snow (see Rule 131).

62.   Watch out for snow-ploughs which may throw out snow on either side. Do not overtake them unless the lane you intend to use has been cleared of snow.

The safety of pedestrians

63.   Show consideration to pedestrians. Drive carefully and slowly when there are pedestrians about, especially in crowded shopping streets or residential areas and near bus and tram stops, parked milk floats or mobile shops. Watch out for pedestrians emerging suddenly into the road, especially from behind parked vehicles.

64. Watch out for children and elderly pedestrians who may not be able to judge your speed and could step into the road in front of you. Watch out for blind and partially sighted people who may be carrying white sticks (white with two red reflective bands for deaf and blind people) or using guide dogs and for people with other disabilities. Give them plenty of time to cross the road. Do not assume that a pedestrian can hear your vehicle coming; they may have hearing difficulties.

65. Drive slowly near schools. In some places, there may be a flashing amber signal below the 'School' warning sign which tells you that there may be children crossing the road ahead. When these signals are flashing, drive very slowly until you are well clear of the area. Drive carefully when passing a stationary bus showing a 'School Bus' sign (see page 60) as children may be getting on or off.

66. You **MUST** stop when a school crossing patrol shows a 'STOP–CHILDREN' sign.

67. Be careful near a parked ice-cream van – children are more interested in ice-cream than in traffic.

68. At road junctions, give way to pedestrians

Watch out for children.

who are already crossing the road into which you are turning.

69. Give way to pedestrians on a pavement you need to cross, eg to reach a driveway.

Remember: pavements are for people – not for vehicles

70. Be prepared for pedestrians walking in the road, especially on narrow country roads. Give them plenty of room. Take extra care on left-hand bends and keep your speed down.

Pedestrian crossings
71. As you approach a Zebra crossing, look out for people waiting to cross (especially children, elderly people or people with disabilities). Be ready to slow down or stop to let them cross. When someone has stepped on to a crossing, you **MUST** give way. Allow more time for stopping on wet or icy roads. Do not wave people across; this could be dangerous if another vehicle is approaching.

72. You **MUST NOT** overtake or park on a Zebra or Pelican crossing, including the area marked by zig-zag lines. Even when there are no zig-zags, do not overtake just before the crossing.

Keep pedestrian crossings clear.

73. In a queue of traffic, you **MUST** keep pedestrian crossings clear.

74. At Pelican crossings a flashing amber light will follow the red 'STOP' light. When the amber light is flashing, you **MUST** give way to any pedestrians on the crossing. A Pelican crossing which goes straight across the road is one crossing even when there is a central island and you **MUST** wait for pedestrians crossing from the other side of the island. Do not harass pedestrians – for example, by revving your engine.

Give way to pedestrians.

75. At pedestrian crossings controlled by lights, give way to pedestrians who are still crossing after the signal for vehicles has changed to green.

Emergency vehicles
76. Look and listen for ambulances, fire engines, police or other emergency vehicles with flashing blue lights or sirens. Make room for them to pass (if necessary by pulling to the side of the road and stopping) but do not endanger other road users. A flashing green light on a vehicle indicates a doctor answering an emergency call so give way as soon as possible.

Flashing amber lights on vehicles
77. Drive carefully when you see a flashing amber light as it warns of a slow-moving vehicle (such as a road gritter or tractor) or a vehicle which has broken down.

Police stopping procedures
78. If the police want to stop your vehicle they will, where possible, attract your attention from behind by flashing their headlights or blue light or

by sounding their siren or horn. A police officer will direct you to pull over to the side by pointing and using the left indicator. You **MUST** pull over and stop as soon as it is safe to do so and then switch off your engine.

Buses

79. Give way to buses whenever you can do so safely, especially when they signal to pull away from bus stops. Look out for people leaving the bus and crossing the road.

Animals

80. Watch out for animals being led or ridden on the road and take extra care at left-hand bends and on narrow country roads. Drive slowly past animals. Give them plenty of room and be ready to stop. Do not scare animals by sounding your horn or revving your engine.

81. Look out for horse riders' signals and be aware that they may not move to the centre of the road prior to turning right. Riders of horses and ponies are often children – so take extra care.

Single-track roads

82. Some roads (often called single-track roads) are only wide enough for one vehicle. They may have special passing places. Pull into a passing place on your left, or wait opposite a passing place on your right, when you see a vehicle coming towards you, or the driver behind you wants to overtake. Give way to vehicles coming uphill whenever you can. Do not park in passing places.

LINES AND LANES ALONG THE ROAD

83. A single broken line, with long markings and short gaps, along the centre of the road is a hazard warning line (see page 63). Do not cross it unless you can see that the road is clear well ahead.

84. Where there are double white lines along the road and the line nearest to you is unbroken, you **MUST NOT** cross or straddle it unless you need to get in or out of property or a side road, or avoid something stationary blocking your lane.

85.   Where there are double white lines along the road and the line nearest to you is broken, you may cross the lines to overtake if it is safe, provided you can do so before reaching an unbroken white line on your side.

86.   Areas of white diagonal stripes or white chevrons painted on the road are to separate traffic lanes or to protect traffic turning right. Where the marked area is bordered by an unbroken white line, you **MUST NOT** enter it except in an emergency. Where the line is broken, you should not enter the area unless you can see that it is safe to do so.

87.   Short broken white lines divide the road into lanes – keep between them. Coloured reflecting road studs may be used with white lines – white studs to mark the lanes or middle of the road, red studs to mark the left edge of the road and amber studs by the central reservation of a dual carriageway. Green studs may be used across lay-bys and side roads.

88.   On some hills an extra uphill 'crawler' lane may be provided. Use this lane if you are driving a slow moving vehicle or if there are vehicles behind you wishing to overtake.

Lane discipline
89.   If you need to change lane, first use your mirrors to make sure you will not force another driver or rider to swerve or slow down. If it is safe to move over, signal before you do so.

Remember: mirrors–signal–manoeuvre

90.   At some junctions, lanes may go in different directions. Follow the signs and get into the correct lane in good time.

91.   In a traffic hold-up, do not try to 'jump the queue' by cutting into another lane or by overtaking the vehicles in front of you.

92.   Where a single carriageway has three lanes and the road markings do not give priority to traffic in either direction, use the middle lane only for overtaking or turning right. Remember – you have no more right to use the middle lane than a driver coming from the opposite direction. Do not use the right-hand lane.

93.   Where a single carriageway has four or more lanes, do not use the lanes on the right-hand side of the road unless signs and markings indicate that you can.

94.   On a two-lane dual carriageway, use the right-hand lane only for overtaking or turning right.

95.   On a three-lane dual carriageway, stay in the left-hand lane. If there are slower vehicles than you in that lane, use the middle lane to overtake them but return to the left-hand lane when it is clear. The right-hand lane is for overtaking (or turning right); if you use it for overtaking, move back into the middle lane and then into the left-hand lane as soon as it is safe to do so.

Choose the correct lane.

96.   In one-way streets, choose the correct lane for your exit as soon as you can. Do not change lanes suddenly. Unless road signs or markings indicate otherwise, choose the left-hand lane when going to the left, the right-hand lane when going to the right and the most appropriate lane when going straight ahead. Remember – traffic could be passing on both sides.

97.   Bus and tram lanes are shown by road

markings and signs. You **MUST NOT** drive in a tram lane or in a bus lane during its period of operation unless the signs indicate you may do so.

98. Cycle lanes are shown by road markings and signs. You **MUST NOT** drive or park in a cycle lane marked by an unbroken white line during its period of operation. Do not drive in a cycle lane marked by a broken white line unless it is unavoidable.

OVERTAKING

99. Do not overtake unless you can do so safely. Make sure the road is sufficiently clear ahead and behind. Do not get too close to the vehicle you intend to overtake – it will obscure your view of the road ahead. Use your mirrors. Signal before you start to move out. Take extra care at night and in poor visibility when it is harder to judge speed and distance.

Remember: mirrors–signal–manoeuvre

100. Once you have started to overtake, quickly move past the vehicle you are overtaking, leaving it plenty of room. Then move back to the left as soon as you can but do not cut in.

Give riders plenty of room when overtaking.

101. When overtaking motorcyclists, pedal-cyclists or horse riders, give them at least as much room as you would give a car. Remember that cyclists may be unable to ride in a straight line, especially when it is windy or the road surface is uneven.

102. Do not overtake on the left unless:

- the vehicle in front is signalling to turn right, and you can overtake on the left safely;
- traffic is moving slowly in queues and vehicles in a lane on the right are moving more slowly than you are.

103. In slow-moving traffic queues, move to a lane on your left only to turn left. Do not change lanes to the left to overtake. Cyclists and motorcyclists overtaking traffic queues should watch out for pedestrians crossing between vehicles and vehicles emerging from junctions.

104. Do not increase your speed when you are being overtaken. Slow down if necessary to let the overtaking vehicle pass and pull in.

105. On a two-lane single carriageway give way to vehicles coming towards you before passing parked vehicles or other obstructions on your side of the road.

106. **a** You **MUST NOT** overtake:

- if you would have to cross or straddle double white lines with an unbroken line nearest to you;
- if you are in the zig-zag area at a pedestrian crossing;
- after a 'No Overtaking' sign and until you pass a sign cancelling the restriction;

b **DO NOT** overtake:

i) where you cannot see far enough ahead to be sure it is safe, for example when you are approaching or at:
- a corner or bend;
- a hump bridge;
- the brow of a hill; or

ii) where you might come into conflict with other road users, for example:
- approaching or at a road junction on either side of the road;
- where the road narrows;

- when approaching a school crossing patrol;
- where you would have to drive over an area marked with diagonal stripes or chevrons;
- where you would have to enter a lane reserved for buses, trams or cyclists;
- between a bus or tram and the kerb when it is at a stop;
- where traffic is queuing at junctions or road works;
- when you would force another vehicle to swerve or slow down;
- at a level crossing.

If in doubt – do not overtake

ROAD JUNCTIONS

107. Take extra care at junctions. Check your position and speed. Junctions are particularly dangerous for cyclists, motorcyclists and pedestrians, so watch out for them before you turn. Watch out for long vehicles which may be turning at a junction ahead; they may have to use the whole width of the road to make the turn.

Give way to pedestrians.

108. Give way to pedestrians crossing a road into which you are turning.

109. At a junction with a 'STOP' sign and an unbroken white line across the road, you **MUST** stop behind the line. Wait for a safe gap in the traffic before you move off.

110. At a junction with broken white lines across the road (it may also have a 'Give Way' sign or a triangle marked on the road), you **MUST** give way to traffic on the other road.

111. When waiting at a junction, do not assume that a vehicle coming from the right and signalling left will do so. Wait and make sure.

112. When going straight across or turning right into a dual carriageway, treat each half as a separate road. Wait in the central reservation until there is a safe gap in the traffic on the second half of the road. If the central reservation is too narrow for the length of your vehicle, wait until you can cross both carriageways in one go.

113. Box junctions have criss-cross yellow lines painted on the road (see page 65). You **MUST NOT** enter the box until your exit road or lane from it is clear. But you may enter the box when you want to turn right and are only stopped from doing so by oncoming traffic or by vehicles waiting to turn right.

Do not go forward unless you can clear the junction.

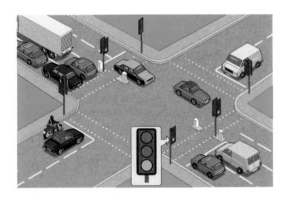

Junctions controlled by traffic lights

114. At junctions controlled by traffic lights, you **MUST** stop behind the white 'STOP' line across your side of the road unless the light is green. You **MUST NOT** move forward when the red and amber lights are showing. Do not go forward when the traffic lights are green unless there is room for you to clear the junction safely or you are taking up a position to turn right.

115. Where traffic lights have a green filter arrow indicating a filter only lane, do not enter that lane unless you want to go in the direction of the arrow. Give other traffic, especially cyclists, room to move into the correct lane.

116. If the traffic lights are not working, proceed with caution.

Turning right
117. Well before you turn right, use your mirrors to make sure you know the position and movement of traffic behind you. Give a right-turn signal and, as soon as it is safe for you to do so, take up a position just left of the middle of the road or in the space marked for right-turning traffic. If possible leave room for other vehicles to pass on the left. Wait until there is a safe gap between you and any oncoming vehicle. Watch out for cyclists, motorcyclists and pedestrians; then make the turn, but do not cut the corner. Take great care when turning into a main road; you will need to watch for traffic in both directions and wait for a safe gap.

Remember: mirrors–signal–manoeuvre

Turn offside-to-offside if possible.

118. When turning right at a junction where an oncoming vehicle is also turning right, it is normally safer to keep the other vehicle to your right and turn behind it: ie offside-to-offside. Before you complete the turn, check for other traffic on the road you want to cross.

Take care when turning nearside-to-nearside.

119. If the lay-out of the junction or the traffic situation makes offside-to-offside passing impracticable, pass nearside-to-nearside, but take care. The other vehicle could obstruct your view of the road so watch carefully for oncoming traffic.

120. When turning right from a dual carriageway, wait in the opening in the central reservation until you are sure it is safe to cross the other carriageway.

Turning left

121. Well before you turn left, use your mirrors and give a left-turn signal. Do not overtake a cyclist, motorcyclist or horse rider immediately before turning left and watch out for traffic coming up on your left before you make the turn. When turning, keep as close to the left as it is safe to do so.

Wait for a safe gap before turning.

122. If you want to turn left across a bus lane, cycle lane or tramway, give way to any vehicles using it from either direction.

ROUNDABOUTS

123. On approaching a roundabout, decide as early as possible which exit you need to take and get into the correct lane. Reduce your speed. On reaching the roundabout, give way to traffic on your right unless road markings indicate otherwise. Watch out for traffic already on the roundabout, especially cyclists and motorcyclists. At some junctions there may be more than one roundabout. At each one, use the normal rules for roundabouts.

124. Unless signs or road markings indicate otherwise:

● When turning left:
  - signal left and approach in the left-hand lane;
  - keep to the left on the roundabout and continue signalling left.

- When going straight ahead:
  - do not signal on approach;
  - approach in the left-hand or centre lane on a three-lane road (on a two-lane road you may approach in the right-hand lane if the left-hand lane is blocked);
  - take the same course on the roundabout;
  - signal left after you have passed the exit before the one you want.
- When turning right or going full circle:
  - signal right and approach in the right-hand lane;
  - keep to the right on the roundabout;
  - continue to signal right until you have passed the exit before the one you want, then signal left.

When there are more than three lanes at the entrance to a roundabout, use the most appropriate lane on approach and through the roundabout.

125.   Watch out for traffic crossing in front of you on the roundabout, especially vehicles intending to leave by the next exit. Show them consideration.

126.   Watch out for motorcyclists, cyclists and horse riders. Give them plenty of room. Cyclists and horse riders will often keep to the left on the roundabout; they may also indicate right to show they are continuing around the roundabout.

127.   Long vehicles may have to take a different course, both approaching and on the roundabout. Watch for their signals and give them plenty of room.

Follow the correct procedure at roundabouts.

128. The same rules apply to mini-roundabouts. If possible, pass around the central marking. Watch out for vehicles making a U-turn and for long vehicles which may have to cross the centre of the mini-roundabout.

Follow the correct procedure at roundabouts.

REVERSING

129. Before reversing make sure there are no pedestrians – particularly children – or obstructions in the road behind you. Be aware of the 'blind spot' behind you – the part of the road you cannot see from the driving seat. Reverse with care. If you cannot see clearly, get someone to guide you. You **MUST NOT** reverse your vehicle for longer than necessary.

Reverse with care.

130. **NEVER** reverse from a side-road into a main road. Avoid reversing into the road from a driveway; where possible, reverse in and drive out.

VEHICLE LIGHTS

131. You **MUST**:

- make sure all your lights are clean, that they work and that your headlights are properly adjusted – badly adjusted headlights can dazzle other road users and may cause accidents;
- use sidelights between sunset and sunrise;
- use headlights at night (between half an hour after sunset and half an hour before sunrise) on all roads without street lighting and on roads where the street lights are more than 185 metres (600 ft) apart or are not lit;
- use headlights or front fog lights when visibility is seriously reduced, generally when you cannot see for more than 100 metres (328 ft).

132. You should also:

- use headlights at night on lit motorways and roads with a speed limit in excess of 50 mph;
- use dipped headlights at night in built-up areas unless the road is well lit;
- cut down glare. If your vehicle has dim-dip, use it instead of dipped headlights in dull daytime weather and at night in built-up areas with good street lighting;
- dip your headlights when meeting vehicles or other road users and before you dazzle the driver of a vehicle you are following;
- slow down or stop if you are dazzled by oncoming headlights.

Fog lights
133. Use fog lights when visibility is seriously reduced, generally when you cannot see for more than 100 metres (328 ft). You **MUST NOT** use fog lights at other times. Remember to switch them off when visibility improves.

Hazard warning lights

134. Hazard warning lights may be used when your vehicle is stopped to warn that it is temporarily obstructing traffic. You may only use them whilst driving if you are on a motorway or unrestricted dual carriageway and you need to warn drivers behind you of a hazard or obstruction ahead. Only use them for just long enough to ensure that your warning has been observed. Never use them as an excuse for dangerous or illegal parking.

Flashing headlights

135. Flashing your headlights means only one thing – it lets another road user know you are there. Do not flash your headlights for any other reason and never assume that it is a signal to proceed.

Use of the horn

136. When your vehicle is moving, use your horn only if you need to warn other road users of your presence. Never sound your horn aggressively. You **MUST NOT** use your horn;

- between 11.30 pm and 7.00 am in a built-up area;
- when your vehicle is stationary, unless a moving vehicle poses a danger.

WAITING AND PARKING

137. Wherever possible, pull off the road on to an area provided for parking. If you have to stop on the road, stop as close as you can to the side. Leave plenty of room when parking next to or behind a vehicle displaying a disabled person's badge. Before you or your passengers open a door, make sure it will not hit anyone passing on the road or pavement or force them to swerve; watch out particularly for pedestrians, cyclists and motorcyclists. It is safer for you and your passengers (especially children) to get out on the side next to the kerb. You **MUST** switch off the engine and headlights. Before leaving the vehicle, ensure that the handbrake is on firmly. Always lock your vehicle.

138. You **MUST NOT** stop or park on:

- the carriageway of a motorway (see Rules 179–180);
- a pedestrian crossing, including the area marked by the zig-zag lines (see Rule 72);
- a Clearway (see page 58);
- an Urban Clearway within its hours of operation except to pick up or set down passengers (see page 58);
- a road marked with double white lines even if one of the lines is broken, except to pick up or set down passengers;
- a bus, tram or cycle lane during its period of operation.

139. You **MUST NOT** park where there are parking restrictions shown by yellow lines along the edge of the carriageway (see page 64), or red lines in the case of specially designated 'red routes'. The periods when restrictions apply are indicated by signs either adjacent to the kerb or on entry to a controlled parking zone. Use an authorised parking space if one is available.

140. Think before you park. **DO NOT** park your vehicle where it would endanger or inconvenience pedestrians or other road users, for example:

- on a footpath, pavement or cycle track;
- near a school entrance;
- at or near a bus stop or taxi rank;
- on the approach to a level crossing;
- within 10 metres (32 ft) of a junction, except in an authorised parking space;
- near the brow of a hill or hump bridge;
- opposite a traffic island or (if this would cause an obstruction) another parked vehicle;
- where you would force other traffic to enter a tram lane;
- where the kerb has been lowered to help wheelchair users;
- in front of the entrance to a property.

141. You **MUST NOT** park in a parking space reserved for specific users, such as Orange Badge holders or residents, unless entitled to do so.

Parking at night

142. You **MUST NOT** park at night facing against the direction of the traffic flow.

143. When parking on the road at night, you **MUST** leave your sidelights on. However cars, goods vehicles not exceeding 1525kg unladen, invalid carriages and motorcycles may be parked without lights on a road with a speed limit of 30 mph or less if they are:

- at least 10 metres (32 ft) away from any junction, close to the kerb and facing in the direction of the traffic flow; or
- in a recognised parking place.

Other vehicles and trailers, and all vehicles with projecting loads, **MUST NOT** be left on a road at night without lights.

Parking in fog

144. It is especially dangerous to park on the road in fog. If it is unavoidable, leave your sidelights on.

Loading and unloading

145. Restrictions on loading and unloading are shown by yellow markings on the kerb (see page 64). Loading and unloading may be permitted when parking is otherwise restricted.

146. Goods vehicles with a maximum laden weight of over 7.5 tonnes (including any trailer) **MUST NOT** be parked on a central reservation without police permission or on a verge or footway, except where this is essential for loading or unloading (in which case the vehicle **MUST NOT** be left unattended).

ROAD WORKS

147. Special care is needed at road works. Watch out for and act on all signs on the approach to and at road works. Use your mirrors and get into the correct lane for your vehicle in good time. Do not switch lanes to overtake queuing traffic or drive through an area marked off by traffic cones. Watch out for traffic entering or leaving the works area, but do not be distracted by what is going on there.

148. You **MUST NOT** exceed any temporary maximum speed limit.

BREAKDOWNS AND ACCIDENTS

149. If you have a breakdown, think first of other traffic. Get your vehicle off the road if possible.

150. If your vehicle is causing an obstruction, warn other traffic by using your hazard warning lights. If you carry a red warning triangle, put it on the road at least 50 metres (164 ft) before the obstruction and on the same side of the road (150 metres [492 ft] on the hard shoulder of motorways). At night or in poor visibility, do not stand behind your vehicle or let anyone else do so – you could prevent other drivers seeing your rear lights.

151. If anything falls from your vehicle on to the road, stop and retrieve it as soon as it is safe to do so (for motorways see Rule 178).

152. If you see warning signs or the flashing lights of emergency vehicles or vehicles in the distance moving very slowly or stopped, there could have been an accident. Slow down and be ready to stop. Do not be distracted when passing the accident; you could cause another one.

153. If you are involved in, or stop to give assistance at, an accident:

- warn other traffic, eg by switching on your hazard warning lights. Ask drivers to switch off their engines and put out any cigarettes;
- arrange for the emergency services to be called immediately with full details of the accident location and any casualties; on a motorway, use the emergency telephone;
- do not move injured people from their vehicles unless they are in immediate danger from fire or explosion. Do not remove a motorcyclist's

helmet unless it is essential. Be prepared to give first aid as shown on pages 75 and 76;

- move uninjured people away from the vehicles to safety; on a motorway this should be well away from the traffic, the hard shoulder and the central reservation;
- stay at the scene until emergency services arrive.

Accidents involving dangerous goods

154. Vehicles carrying dangerous goods in packages will be marked with plain orange reflectorised plates. Road tankers and vehicles carrying tank containers will have hazard warning plates (see page 66). If an accident involves a vehicle containing dangerous goods, follow the advice in Rule 153 and, in particular:

- switch off engines and **DO NOT SMOKE**;
- keep uninjured people well away from the vehicle and where the wind will not blow dangerous substances towards them. Even if you act to save a life, take care that you too are not affected by dangerous substances;
- give the emergency services as much information as possible about the labels and other markings.

 **MOTORWAYS**

Many other Rules also apply to motorway driving, either wholly or in part: Rules 28–35, 39–49, 51, 52, 54, 56–62, 76–78, 87, 89–91, 94, 95, 131–136, 138, 147–150, 152–154 and 213.

GENERAL

155. Motorways **MUST NOT** be used by pedestrians, provisional licence holders, riders of motorcycles under 50cc, cyclists and horse riders. Slow-moving vehicles, agricultural vehicles and some invalid carriages are also prohibited. (See page 71.)

156. Traffic on motorways travels more quickly than on other roads, so you have to think quickly too. It is especially important to use your mirrors earlier and look much further ahead than you would on other roads.

157. Make sure your vehicle is fit to cruise at speed, has correct tyre pressures and enough fuel, oil and water to get you at least to the next service area. See that the windscreen, windows, mirrors, lights and reflectors are clean and that the windscreen washer bottle is topped up. You **MUST** make sure that any load you are carrying or towing is secure.

JOINING THE MOTORWAY

158. When you join the motorway you will normally approach it from a road on the left (a slip-road). You **MUST** give way to traffic already on the motorway. While on the slip-road, check the traffic already on the motorway and adjust your speed so that you join the left-hand lane where there is a safe gap and at the same speed as traffic in that lane.

159. At some junctions the slip-road will continue as an extra lane on the motorway. Where signs indicate that this will happen, stay in that lane until it becomes part of the motorway.

160. After joining the motorway, stay in the left-hand lane long enough to get used to the speed of traffic before overtaking.

ON THE MOTORWAY

161. When you can see well ahead and the road conditions are good, drive at a steady cruising speed which you and your vehicle can handle easily. You **MUST NOT** exceed the maximum speed limit for your vehicle (see page 53). Keep a safe distance from the vehicle in front and increase the gap on wet or icy roads, or in fog (see Rules 57–58).

162. Driving can make you feel sleepy. To help prevent this, make sure there is a supply of fresh air into your vehicle, stop at a service area or leave the motorway and find a safe place to stop.

163. You **MUST NOT** reverse, cross the central reservation, or drive against the traffic flow. Even if you have missed your exit, or have taken the wrong route, carry on to the next exit.

Lane discipline
164. Keep in the left-hand lane unless overtaking. You may use the lane to the right of a stream of slower vehicles to overtake them but return to the lane to your left when you have passed them.

165. When approaching a junction make sure you are in the correct lane; at some junctions a lane may lead directly off the motorway.

166. Some vehicles **MUST NOT** use the right-hand lane of a motorway with three or more lanes (see page 71).

Overtaking
167. Overtake only on the right unless traffic is moving in queues and the queue on your right is moving more slowly than you are. Do not move to a lane on your left to overtake. You **MUST NOT** use the hard shoulder for overtaking.

Do not get too close to the vehicle you are going to overtake.

168. Do not overtake unless you are sure it is safe to do so. Before you start to overtake, make sure that the lane you will be joining is sufficiently clear ahead and behind. Use your mirrors.

Remember that traffic may be coming up behind you very quickly. Signal before you move out. Be especially careful at night and in poor visibility when it is harder to judge speed and distance.

169.   Always get back to the left-hand lane or, if it is occupied, the middle lane, as soon as you can after overtaking. Signal your intention to change lanes. Do not cut in on the vehicle you have overtaken.

Remember: mirrors–signal–manoeuvre

Motorway signals
170.   Motorway signals (see page 54) are used to warn you of a danger ahead, for example an accident or risk of skidding. Usually they are situated on the central reservation where they apply to all lanes. On very busy stretches, they may be overhead with a signal for each lane.

171.   Where there is danger, amber lights flash. The signal may also show a temporary maximum speed limit, lanes that are closed or a message (for example, 'Fog'). Reduce your speed and look out for the danger until you pass a signal which is not flashing and you are sure it is safe to increase your speed.

172.   If red lights on the overhead signals flash above your lane (there may also be a red X), you **MUST NOT** go beyond the signal in that lane. If red lights flash on a signal in the central reservation or a slip-road, you **MUST NOT** go beyond the signal in any lane.

Pay attention to motorway signals.

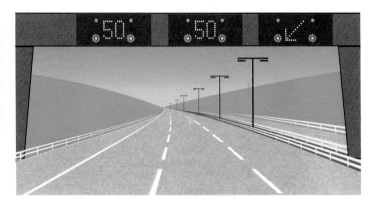

40

173. All signals are there to protect you. Always do what they say. Remember – danger, such as drifting fog, may be there even if you cannot immediately see the cause.

Road studs and signs
174. To help drivers on motorways at night, there are amber-coloured studs marking the right-hand edge of the road, red studs marking the left-hand edge and green studs separating the slip-road from the motorway. White studs separate the lanes on the motorway.

175. On some motorways, direction signs are placed over the road. If you need to change lanes, do so in good time.

Fog
176. When driving in fog, obey the fog code (see Rule 58).

Road works
177. Take special care at road works (see Rules 147–148). One or more lanes may be closed to traffic and a lower speed limit may apply. Keep a safe distance from the vehicle in front (see Rule 57).

Obstructions
178. If anything that could be dangerous falls from your vehicle or any other vehicle, stop at the next emergency telephone to tell the police. Do not try to remove it yourself.

Stopping and parking
179. You **MUST NOT** stop except:
- in an emergency;
- when told to do so by the police, by an emergency sign or by flashing red light signals.

180. You **MUST NOT** park on:
- the carriageway;
- the slip-road;
- the hard shoulder;
- the central reservation.

181. You **MUST NOT** pick up or set down anyone on a slip-road or on any other part of the motorway.

182. You **MUST NOT** walk on the carriageway except in an emergency.

Breakdowns
183. If your vehicle develops a problem, leave the motorway at the next exit or pull into a service area. If you cannot do so, you should:
- try to stop near an emergency telephone (you will find them at one mile intervals along the hard shoulder);
- pull on to the hard shoulder and stop as far to the left as possible;
- switch on your hazard warning lights;
- keep your sidelights on if it is dark or visibility is poor;
- leave the vehicle by the left-hand door and ensure your passengers do the same (leave any animals inside);
- ensure passengers wait near the vehicle, but well away from the carriageway and hard shoulder, and that children are kept under control;
- walk to an emergency telephone (following the arrows on the posts at the back of the hard shoulder) – it is free to use and connects directly to the police. Give full details to the police – tell them if you are a woman travelling alone – and then return to your vehicle;
- wait near your vehicle but well away from the carriageway and hard shoulder. If you feel at risk, return to your vehicle by a left-hand door and lock all doors. Leave your vehicle again as soon as you feel the danger has passed.

If you cannot get your vehicle on to the hard shoulder:
- switch on your hazard warning lights;
- leave your vehicle only if you are sure you can safely get clear of the carriageway;
- if in doubt, remain in your vehicle wearing a seat belt until the emergency services arrive;
- do not attempt to place a warning triangle on the carriageway.

If you have a disability which prevents you from following the above advice:
- stay in your vehicle with all doors locked;
- switch on your hazard warning lights;

- display a 'Help' pennant or, if you have a car telephone, contact the emergency services.

Do not attempt even simple repairs and remember you **MUST NOT** try to cross the motorway.

184. Before rejoining the carriageway, build-up speed on the hard shoulder and watch for a safe gap in the traffic.

LEAVING THE MOTORWAY

185. Unless signs indicate that a lane leads directly off the motorway, you will leave the motorway by a slip-road on your left. Watch for the signs letting you know you are getting near your exit. If you are not already in the left-hand lane, move into it well before reaching your exit and stay in it. Signal left in good time and slow down as necessary.

186. When leaving the motorway or using a link road between motorways, your speed may be higher than you think – 50 mph may feel like 30 mph. Check your speedometer and adjust your speed accordingly. Some slip-roads and link roads have sharp bends so you will need to slow down.

EXTRA RULES FOR CYCLISTS

CHOOSING AND MAINTAINING YOUR CYCLE

187. Choose the right size of cycle for comfort and safety.

188. Make sure that the:
- lights and reflectors are kept clean and in good working order;

- tyres are in good condition and inflated to the pressure recommended by the cycle manufacturer;
- brakes and gears are working correctly;
- chain is properly adjusted and oiled;
- saddle is adjusted to the correct height.

189. Fit a bell and use it when necessary to warn other road users, particularly blind and partially sighted pedestrians, that you are there.

Wear clothes which will help you to be seen.

SAFETY EQUIPMENT AND CLOTHING

190. Wear a cycle helmet which conforms to recognised safety standards. Choose appropriate clothes for cycling. Avoid long coats or other clothes which may get tangled in the chain or a wheel. Light-coloured or fluorescent clothing helps other road users see you in daylight and poor visibility.

191. At night you **MUST** use front and rear lights and a red rear reflector. Reflective material such as belts, arm and ankle bands, wheel reflectors and 'spacer' flags will also help you to be seen at night.

192. You **MUST** obey traffic signs and traffic light signals (see pages 54, 58 and 59). You **MUST NOT** cycle on the pavement.

193. Look all around before moving away from the kerb, turning or manoeuvring to make sure it is safe to do so. Then give a clear arm signal to show other road users what you intend to do.

194. Look well ahead for obstructions in the road, such as drains, pot-holes and parked cars so that you do not have to swerve suddenly to avoid them. Leave plenty of room when passing parked cars and watch out for doors being opened into your path.

195. Take care near road humps, narrowings and other traffic calming features. Do not ride along a drainage channel at the edge of the road to avoid such features.

196. Do not leave your cycle where it would endanger or obstruct other road users, for example lying on the pavement. Use cycle parking facilities where provided.

Road junctions
197. Watch out for vehicles turning in front of you from or into a side road. Do not overtake on the left of vehicles slowing down to turn left. Pay particular attention to long vehicles which need a lot of room to manoeuvre at corners and may have to move over to the right before turning left. Wait until they have completed the manoeuvre.

198. When turning right, check the traffic behind you, signal and when it is safe move to the centre of the road. Wait until there is a safe gap in traffic before completing the turn. It may be safer to wait on the left until there is a safe gap or to dismount and walk your cycle across the road.

Signal controlled junctions
199. Traffic signals also apply to cyclists. You **MUST NOT** cross the stop line across the road

when the lights are red. Some junctions have advanced stop lines which enable cyclists to position themselves ahead of other traffic. Where these are provided, use them.

Roundabouts

200. Rules 123–128 set out the correct procedures at roundabouts but you may feel safer approaching in the left-hand lane and keeping to the left in the roundabout. If you do keep to the left, take extra care when cycling across exits and signal right to show you are not leaving. Watch out for vehicles crossing your path to leave or join the roundabout.

201. Watch out for long vehicles on the roundabout as they need more space to manoeuvre. It may be safer to wait until they have cleared the roundabout.

202. If you are unsure about using the roundabout, dismount and walk your cycle round on the pavement or verge.

Bus lanes

203. You may only use a bus lane if the signs include a cycle symbol. Be very careful when overtaking a bus or leaving a bus lane as you will be entering a busier traffic flow.

Dual carriageways

204. Take great care when crossing or turning on to a dual carriageway where there are no traffic light signals. Wait for safe gaps and cross each carriageway in turn. Remember that traffic on most dual carriageways travels quickly.

Cycle lanes and tracks

205. Use cycle lanes and tracks wherever possible. They can make your journey safer and quicker.

206. Cycle lanes are marked by either an unbroken or broken white line along the carriageway (see Rule 98). Keep within the lane and watch out for traffic emerging from side turnings.

207. Cycle tracks are located away from the road. Where a cycle track is shared with a footpath, you **MUST** keep to the track intended for cyclists. Watch out for pedestrians, especially elderly people and people with disabilities, using the footpath or crossing the cycle track.

208. Cycle tracks on opposite sides of the road are sometimes linked by signalled crossings. If the crossing is provided for cyclists only, you may ride across but you **MUST NOT** cross until the green cycle symbol is showing. Do not ride across a Pelican crossing.

Safe riding
209. When cycling:

- keep both hands on the handlebars except when signalling or changing gear;
- keep both feet on the pedals;
- do not ride more than two abreast;
- ride in single file on cycle tracks and lanes, and on narrow roads when in traffic;
- do not ride close behind another vehicle;
- do not carry anything which will affect your balance or may get tangled up with your wheels or chain.

210. You **MUST NOT** carry a passenger unless your cycle has been built or adapted to carry one.

211. You **MUST NOT** ride under the influence of drink or drugs.

ANIMALS

GENERAL

212. Do not let your dog out on its own. Keep it on a short lead when taking it for a walk on or near a road or on a path shared with cyclists.

213. Keep animals under control in vehicles. Make sure they cannot distract you while you are driving. Do not let a dog out of a vehicle on to the road unless it is on a lead.

214. If you are herding animals, keep to the left of the road; if possible, send another person along the road to warn other road users, for example at bends and the brows of hills.

215. If you have to herd animals after dark, wear reflective clothing and ensure that white lights are carried at the front and red lights at the rear of the herd.

HORSE RIDERS

216. Before you take a horse on to a road, make sure you can control it. If you think that your horse will be nervous of traffic, always ride with other, less nervous, horses.

217. Make sure all tack fits well and is in good condition. Never ride a horse without a saddle or bridle.

218. Wear an approved safety helmet and fasten it securely – children under the age of 14 **MUST** do this. You should also wear boots or shoes with hard soles and heels.

219. If you have to ride at night, wear reflective clothing and make sure your horse has reflective bands on its legs above the fetlock joints. Carry lights which show white to the front and red to the rear.

220. Before riding off or turning, look behind you to make sure it is safe and then give a clear arm signal. When riding, keep to the left. If you are leading a horse, keep it to your left. In one-way streets, move in the direction of the traffic flow.

221. Never ride more than two abreast. Ride in single file on narrow roads.

222. You **MUST NOT** take a horse on to a footpath, pavement or cycle track. Use a bridle-path where possible.

223. Avoid roundabouts wherever possible. If you have to use them, keep to the left and watch out for vehicles crossing your path to leave or join the roundabout. Signal right when riding across exits to show you are not leaving. Signal left just before you leave the roundabout.

224. When riding:

- keep both hands on the reins unless you are signalling;
- keep both feet in the stirrups;
- do not carry another person;
- do not carry anything which might affect your balance or get tangled up with the reins;
- wear light-coloured or fluorescent clothing in daylight and reflective materials at night.

RAILWAY LEVEL CROSSINGS

GENERAL

225. A level crossing is where a road crosses railway lines. Approach and cross it with care. Never drive on to a crossing until the road is clear on the other side – do not drive 'nose to tail' over it. Never stop on or just after a crossing. Never park close to a crossing.

Take care at level crossings: do not zig-zag round the barriers.

226. Most crossings have full or half barriers, traffic light signals with a steady amber light and twin flashing red stop lights (see page 54) and an audible alarm. You **MUST** stop behind the white line across the road when the lights come on. If you have already crossed the white line when the amber lights or audible alarm start, keep going.

227. If a train goes by and the red lights continue to flash or the audible alarm changes tone, you must wait. Another train will be passing soon. It is only safe to cross when the lights go off and any barriers open.

228. At crossings with half barriers, never zig-zag around the barriers. They are lowered because a train is approaching.

Railway telephones
229. If you are driving a large or slow-moving vehicle, or herding animals, you **MUST** obey any sign instructing you to use the railway telephone to obtain permission to cross. You **MUST** also telephone when clear of the crossing.

Accidents and breakdowns
230. If your vehicle breaks down, or if you have an accident on a crossing:

- get everyone out of the vehicle and clear of the crossing;
- if there is a railway telephone, use it immediately to tell the signal operator and follow the instructions you are given;
- if it is possible, and there is time before a train arrives, move the vehicle clear of the crossing. If the alarm sounds, or the amber light comes on, get clear of the crossing.

Crossings without signals
231. At crossings where there are gates or barriers but no lights, stop when they begin to close. Pedestrians should wait at the barrier or gate.

Unattended crossings with signals
232. Some unattended crossings with gates or barriers have 'STOP' signs and small red and green

lights. Do not cross when the red light is on as a train is approaching. Only cross if the green light is on. If crossing with a vehicle, open the gates or barriers on both sides of the crossing, then check that the green light is still on and cross quickly. Close the gates or barriers when you are clear of the crossing.

Unattended crossings without signals

233. Some crossings have gates but no attendant or traffic signals. At such crossings, stop, look both ways, listen and make sure no train is approaching. If there is a railway telephone, contact the signal operator to make sure it is safe to cross. If crossing with a vehicle, open the gates on both sides of the crossing, then check that no train is coming and cross quickly. When you have cleared the crossing, close both gates. Remember to inform the signal operator again when you are clear of the crossing.

Open crossings

234. At an open crossing with no gates, barriers, attendant or traffic lights, there will be a 'Give Way' sign. Look both ways, listen and make sure there is no train coming before you cross. Always 'Give Way' to trains – they cannot stop easily!

TRAMWAYS

GENERAL

235. You **MUST NOT** enter a road or lane reserved for trams. Diamond-shaped signs give instructions to tram drivers only.

236. Take extra care where trams (which can be up to 60 metres [196 ft] in length) run along the road. The area taken up by moving trams is often shown by tram lanes which will be marked by white lines or by a different type of road surface.

237. Take extra care where the track crosses from one side of the road to the other and where the road narrows and the tracks come close to the kerb. There will usually be separate traffic light signals giving instructions to tram drivers and to other traffic. Always give way to trams; do not try to race or overtake them.

238. Where tram stops have platforms, either in the middle or at the side of the road, you **MUST** follow the route shown by the road signs and markings. At stops without platforms, you **MUST NOT** drive between a tram and the left-hand kerb. If a tram is approaching a stop, look out for pedestrians, especially children, running to catch it.

239. You **MUST NOT** park your vehicle where it would get in the way of trams or where it would force other drivers to do so.

240. Cyclists and motorcyclists should take extra care when riding close to or crossing the tracks, especially if the rails are wet.

PEDESTRIANS

241. Where trams run through pedestrian areas, their path will be marked out by shallow kerbs, changes in the road surface or white lines. If the track is unfenced, you may cross at any point. Look both ways and when it is clear, walk straight across; do not walk along the track.

242. Use designated crossing places where provided. Some may have flashing amber lights to warn you that a tram is approaching. Do not start to cross the track when the lights are flashing. If you are already crossing when the lights start to flash, it will be safe to continue. Avoid treading on the rails.

SPEED LIMITS

Type of vehicle	Built-up areas*	Elsewhere		Motorways
	MPH	Single carriage-ways MPH	Dual carriage-ways MPH	MPH
Cars (including car derived vans and motorcycles)	30	60	70	70
Cars towing caravans or trailers (including car derived vans and motorcycles)	30	50	60	60
Buses and coaches (not exceeding 12 metres in overall length)	30	50	60	70
Goods vehicles (not exceeding 7.5 tonnes maximum laden weight)	30	50	60	70†
Goods vehicles (exceeding 7.5 tonnes maximum laden weight)	30	40	50	60

These are the national speed limits and apply to all roads unless signs show otherwise.

* The 30 mph limit applies to all traffic on all roads with street lighting unless signs show otherwise.

† 60 if articulated or towing a trailer

53

LIGHT SIGNALS CONTROLLING TRAFF

TRAFFIC LIGHT SIGNALS

| RED means 'Stop'. Wait behind the stop line on the carriageway. | RED AND AMBER also means 'Stop'. Do not pass through or start until GREEN shows. | GREEN means you may go on if the way is clear. Take special care if you intend to turn left or right and give way to pedestrians who are crossing. | AMBER means 'Stop' at the stop line. You may go on only if the AMBER appears after you have crossed the stop line or are so close to it that to pull up might cause an accident. | A GREEN ARROW may be provided in addition to the full green signal if movement in a certain direction is allowed before or after the full green phase. If the way is clear you may go but only in the direction shown by the arrow. You may do this whatever other lights may be showing. |

FLASHING RED LIGHTS

Alternately flashing red lights mean YOU MUST STOP

At level crossings, lifting bridges, airfields, fire stations etc

MOTORWAY SIGNALS

| Do not proceed further in this lane. | Change lane. | Reduced visibility ahead. | Lane ahead closed. |

 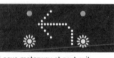

| Temporary maximum speed limit and information message. | Leave motorway at next exit. | Temporary maximum speed limit. | End of restriction. |

LANE CONTROL SIGNALS

Green arrow – lane available to traffic facing the sign. Red crosses – lane closed to traffic facing the sign. White diagonal arrow – change lanes in direction shown.

SIGNALS BY AUTHORISED PERSONS

STOP

Traffic approaching from behind

Traffic approaching from the front

Traffic approaching from both front and behind

BECKONING TRAFFIC ON

Beckoning on traffic from the front

Beckoning on traffic from the side

Beckoning on traffic from behind

SIGNALS TO OTHER ROAD USERS

DIRECTION INDICATOR SIGNALS

I intend to move out to the right or turn right

I intend to move in to the left or turn left or stop on the left

BRAKE LIGHT SIGNALS

I am slowing down or stopping

These signals should not be used except for the purposes described.

ARM SIGNALS

For use when direction indicator signals are not used; or when necessary to reinforce direction indicator signals and stop lights. Also for use by pedal cyclists and those in charge of horses.

I intend to move out to the right or turn right

I intend to move in to the left or turn left

I intend to slow down or stop
This signal is particularly important at Zebra crossings to let other road users, including pedestrians, know that you are slowing down or stopping

ARM SIGNALS TO PERSONS CONTROLLING TRAFFIC

I want to go straight on

I want to turn left

I want to turn right

TRAFFIC SIGNS

SIGNS GIVING ORDERS

These signs are mostly circular and those with red circles are mostly prohibitive.

Entry to
20 mph zone

End of
20 mph zone

School crossing
patrol

Maximum speed

National speed
limit applies

Stop and
give way

Give way to traffic
on major road

No vehicles

No entry for
vehicular traffic

No right turn

No left turn

No U-turns

No
overtaking

Give priority to
vehicles from
opposite
direction

No motor
vehicles

No motor
vehicles except
solo motorcycles,
scooters or
mopeds

Manually operated
temporary 'STOP'
sign

No vehicles with
over 12 seats
except regular
scheduled, school
and work buses

No cycling

No pedestrians

No goods vehicles
over maximum
gross weight
shown (in tonnes)

No vehicle or
combination of
vehicles over
length shown

No vehicles over
height shown

No vehicles over
width shown

No vehicles over
maximum gross
weight shown
(in tonnes)

Axle weight limit
in tonnes

No stopping
(Clearway)

Parking restricted to use
by people named on sign

No stopping during
times shown except
for as long as
necessary to set down
or pick up passengers

Plates below some signs qualify their message

End of
restriction

Exception for
loading/unloading goods

Exception for regular
scheduled, school and
work buses

Exception for access to
premises and land adjacent to
the road where there is no
alternative route

Signs with blue circles but no red border mostly give positive instruction.

One-way traffic (note: compare circular 'Ahead only' sign)

Ahead only

Turn left ahead (right if symbol reversed)

Turn left (right if symbol reversed)

Keep left (right if symbol reversed)

Route to be used by pedal cycles only

Segregated pedal cycle and pedestrian route

Minimum speed

End of minimum speed

Mini-roundabout (roundabout circulation – give way to vehicles from the immediate right)

Vehicles may pass either side to reach same destination

Buses and cycles only

Trams only

Pedestrian crossing point over tramway

With-flow bus and cycle lane

Contra-flow bus lane

With-flow pedal cycle lane

WARNING SIGNS   Mostly triangular

Distance to 'STOP' line ahead

Crossroads

Junction on bend ahead

T-junction

Staggered junction

Distance to 'Give Way' line ahead

Sharp deviation of route to left (or right if chevrons reversed)

Double bend first to left (symbol may be reversed)

Bend to right (or left if symbol reversed)

Roundabout

Uneven road

Plate below some signs

Dual carriageway ends

Road narrows on right (left if symbol reversed)

Road narrows on both sides

Two-way traffic crosses one-way road

Two-way traffic straight ahead

Traffic signals

Failure of traffic light signals

Slippery road

Steep hill downwards

Steep hill upwards

Gradients may be shown as a ratio
i.e. 20% = 1:5

Warning signs – continued

School

Patrol

Children going to
or from school

School crossing
patrol ahead
(Some signs have
amber lights
which flash when
children are
crossing)

Elderly
people

Elderly people (or
blind or disabled as
shown) crossing
road

No footway
for 400 yds

Pedestrians
in road ahead

Pedestrian crossing

Cycle route ahead

Traffic merges from left/right

Road works

Hump bridge

Ford

Worded warning
sign

Loose chippings

Risk of
grounding

STOP
when
lights show

Light signals
ahead at level
crossing, airfield
or bridge

Level crossing
with barrier or gate
ahead

Level crossing
without barrier or
gate ahead

Level crossing
without
barrier

Trams
crossing
ahead

Cattle

Wild animals

Wild horses
or ponies

Accompanied
horses or
ponies

Quayside or
river bank

Opening or
swing bridge
ahead

Low-flying aircraft or
sudden aircraft noise

Falling or
fallen rocks

14'-6"

Available width of headroom
indicated

Safe height
16'-6"

Overhead electric
cable; plate
indicates
maximum height
of vehicles which
can pass safely

1 mile

Distance to
tunnel

Humps for
½ mile

Distance over
which road
humps extend

Hidden dip

Other danger;
plate indicates
nature of
danger

School bus
(Displayed in
front or rear
window of bus
or coach)

DIRECTION SIGNS

Mostly rectangular

Signs on motorways – blue backgrounds

At a junction leading directly into a motorway

On approaches to junctions
(junction number on black backgrounds)

Route confirmatory
sign after junction

Downward pointing arrows mean 'Get in lane'

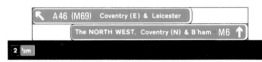

The panel with the sloping arrow indicates the destinations which can be reached by leaving the motorway at the next junction

Signs on primary routes – green backgrounds

On approaches to junctions

On approaches to junctions
(The blue panel indicates that the motorway commences from the junction ahead. The motorway shown in brackets can also be reached by proceeding in that direction)

At the junction

Route confirmatory sign after junction

Airport

Ring road

Signs on non-primary routes – black borders

On approaches to junctions

On approaches to junctions
(A symbol may sometimes be shown to indicate a warning of a hazard or prohibition on a road leading from a junction)

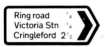

At the junction

Direction to toilets with access for the disabled

Other direction signs

Picnic site

Advisory route for lorries

Symbols showing emergency diversion route for motorway traffic

Ancient monument in the care of English Heritage

Tourist attraction

Route for pedestrians

Direction to camping and caravan site

Holiday route

Diversion route

Recommended route for pedal cycles to place shown

INFORMATION SIGNS — All rectangular

Start of motorway and point from which motorway regulations apply

End of motorway

Tourist information point

Recommended route for pedal cycles

Entrance to controlled parking zone

One-way street

Parking place for towed caravans

Appropriate traffic lanes at junction ahead

End of controlled parking zone

Priority over vehicles from opposite direction

Advanced warning of restriction or prohibition ahead

Temporary lane closure (the number and position of arrows and red bars may be varied according to lanes open and closed)

No through road

Hospital ahead

Motorway service area sign incorporating the operator's name (the current price of petrol may be shown)

'Countdown' markers at exit from motorway (each bar represents 100 yards to the exit). Green-backed markers may be used on primary routes and white-backed markers with red bars on the approaches to concealed level crossings

Bus lane on road at junction ahead

ROAD MARKINGS

ACROSS THE CARRIAGEWAY

Give way to traffic on major road

Give way to traffic from the right in roundabout

Give way to traffic from right at mini-roundabout

Stop line at 'STOP' sign

Stop line at signals or police control

ALONG THE CARRIAGEWAY

Double white lines

Diagonal stripes

Lane markings

See Rules 84 and 85

See Rule 86

Lane line
See Rule 87

Centre
line

Hazard
warning line
See Rule 83

ALONG THE EDGE OF THE CARRIAGEWAY

Waiting restrictions

No waiting on carriageway, pavement or verge (except to load or unload or while passengers board or alight) at times shown on nearby plates or on entry signs to controlled parking zones.

If no days are indicated on the sign, the restrictions are in force every day including Sundays and Bank Holidays. The lines give a guide to the restriction in force but the time plates must be consulted.

Examples of plates indicating restriction times

Continuous prohibition

Plate giving times

Mon - Sat
8am - 6pm
Waiting limited
to 20 minutes
Return prohibited
within 40 minutes

Limited waiting

No waiting for at least eight hours between 7 am and 7 pm on four or more days of the week

No waiting for at least eight hours between 7 am and 7 pm on four or more days of the week plus some additional period outside these times

During any other periods

ON THE KERB OR AT THE EDGE OF THE CARRIAGEWAY

Loading restrictions

No loading or unloading at times shown on nearby plates. If no days are indicated on the sign, the restrictions are in force every day including Sundays and Bank Holidays.

During every working day

For example

No loading
Mon-Sat
8·30am-6·30pm

During every working day, and additional times

For example

No loading
at any time

During any other periods

For example

No loading
Mon-Fri
8·00-9·30am
4·30-6·30pm

64

ZEBRA CONTROLLED AREAS

OTHER ROAD MARKINGS

Keep entrance clear of stationary vehicles, even if picking up or setting down children

Warning of 'Give Way' just ahead

Parking space reserved for vehicles named

See Rule 140

See Rule 97

Box junction
See Rule 113

Do not block entrance to side road

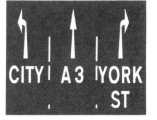

Indication of traffic lanes

Note: Although *The Highway Code* shows many of the signs commonly in use, a comprehensive explanation of our signing system is given in the Department's booklet *Know Your Traffic Signs*, which is on sale at booksellers. The booklet also illustrates and explains the vast majority of signs the road user is likely to encounter. The signs illustrated in *The Highway Code* are not all drawn to the same scale. In Wales, bilingual versions of some signs are used.

VEHICLE MARKINGS

HEAVY GOODS VEHICLE REAR MARKINGS

Motor vehicles over 7500 kilograms maximum gross weight and trailers over 3500 kilograms maximum gross weight

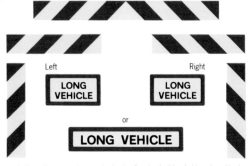

Left

LONG VEHICLE

Right

LONG VEHICLE

or

LONG VEHICLE

The vertical markings are also required to be fitted to builders' skips placed in the road, commercial vehicles or combinations longer than 13 metres (optional on combinations between 11 and 13 metres)

HAZARD WARNING PLATES

Certain tank vehicles carrying dangerous goods must display hazard information panels

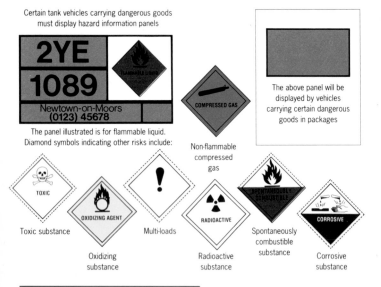

2YE
1089
Newtown-on-Moors
(0123) 45678

FLAMMABLE LIQUID

The panel illustrated is for flammable liquid. Diamond symbols indicating other risks include:

COMPRESSED GAS

Non-flammable compressed gas

The above panel will be displayed by vehicles carrying certain dangerous goods in packages

TOXIC

Toxic substance

OXIDIZING AGENT

Oxidizing substance

!

Multi-loads

RADIOACTIVE

Radioactive substance

SPONTANEOUSLY COMBUSTIBLE

Spontaneously combustible substance

CORROSIVE

Corrosive substance

PROJECTION MARKERS

Side marker

End marker

Both required when load or equipment (eg crane jib) overhangs front or rear by more than two metres

THE ROAD USER AND THE LAW

ROAD TRAFFIC LAW

This section deals with some of the important points of law which affect road safety. It is not intended to be a comprehensive guide. For the precise wording of the law, please refer to the various Acts and Regulations (as amended) indicated in the margin. A list of abbreviations used is given below.

Most of the provisions apply on all roads throughout Great Britain, although there are some exceptions. The definition of a road in England and Wales is 'any highway and any other road to which the public has access and includes bridges over which a road passes'. In Scotland, there is a similar definition which is extended to include any way over which the public have a right of passage. It is important to note that references to 'road' therefore generally include footpaths, bridle-ways and cycle tracks. In most cases, the law will apply to them and there may be additional rules for particular paths or ways. Some serious driving offences, including drink-driving offences, also apply to other public places, for example public car parks.

Road Vehicles (Construction & Use) Regulations 1986	**CUR**
Functions of Traffic Wardens Order 1970	**FTWO**
Highways Act (1835 or 1980, as indicated)	**HA**
Horses (Protective Headgear for Young Riders) Regulations 1992	**H(PHYR)R**
Motor Cycles (Protective Helmets) Regulations 1980	**MC(PH)R**
Motorways Traffic (England & Wales) Regulations 1982	**ME(E&W)R**
Motorways Traffic (England & Wales) (Amendment) Regulations 1992	**MT(E&W)(A)R**
Motorways Traffic (Scotland) Regulations 1964	**MT(S)R**
Motor Vehicles (Driving Licences) Regulations 1987	**MV(DL)R**
Motor Vehicles (Wearing of Seat Belts) Regulations 1993	**MV(WSB)R**
Motor Vehicles (Wearing of Seat Belts by Children in Front Seats) Regulations 1993	**MV(WSBCFS)R**
Pedal Cycles (Construction & Use) Regulations 1983	**PCUR**
'Pelican' Pedestrian Crossing Regulations & General Directions 1987	**PPCRGD**
Roads (Scotland) Act 1984	**R(S)A**
Road Traffic Act 1988	**RTA**
Road Traffic Act (Amendment) Regulations 1992	**RTA(A)R**
Road Traffic Regulation Act 1984	**RTRA**
Road Vehicles Lighting Regulations 1989	**RVLR**
Road Vehicles (Registration & Licensing) Regulations 1971	**RV(R&L)R**
Traffic Signs Regulations & General Directions 1981	**TSRGD**
Vehicles (Excise) Act 1971	**VEA**
'Zebra' Pedestrian Crossings Regulations 1971	**ZPCR**

[E&W = England and Wales; S = Scotland]

A TO DRIVERS OF MOTOR VEHICLES

1. DOCUMENTS: TAX, LICENCE, INSURANCE, ETC
You **MUST** have:

RTA Sect 87

- a **valid driving licence**;

VEA Sects 1 & 12(4)

- a **current vehicle excise licence (tax disc)** which must be displayed on the vehicle;

RTA Sect 143

- valid third party **insurance** covering your use of the vehicle;

RTA Sects 45, 47, 49 & 53

- a current **test certificate (MOT)** if your vehicle is over the prescribed age limit.

2. YOUR VEHICLE

CUR No 100

The law requires that the condition of your vehicle, any trailer it is drawing, its load, and the number of passengers and the way in which they are carried are such that they do not involve danger of injury to yourself or others.

There are more detailed regulations which require the different parts of your vehicle to be kept in good condition and working order. These include **brakes, steering, lights, windscreens and windows, exhaust, seat belts and fittings, speedometer and horn**.

CUR No 27

Tyres MUST have a continuous tread depth of at least 1.6 mm on cars, light vans and light trailers (1 mm for other vehicles) across the centre three-quarters of the width. They **MUST** also be properly inflated and free from cuts and other defects.

RVLR Nos 23 & 27

Headlights MUST be properly adjusted to prevent dazzling oncoming traffic.

CUR Nos 30 & 34

Windscreens and windows MUST be free from obstruction to vision, and **MUST** be kept clean.

3. WEARING OF SEAT BELTS

RTA Sect 14
RTA(A)R No 3105
MV(WSBCFS)R No 31
MV(WSB)R No 176

You and your passengers **MUST** wear a seat belt in the front and (if fitted) the rear of the vehicle, unless you are exempt. Exemptions include the holders of medical exemption certificates, people making local deliveries in a vehicle designed or adapted for that purpose, and children in the rear of taxis with partitions. (See table in Rule 40 of the Code.)

RTA Sect 15
MV(WSBCFS)R No 31
MV(WSB)R No 176

It is the driver's legal responsibility to ensure that children under 14 years comply with the law.

4. FITNESS TO DRIVE

RTA Sect 94

You **MUST** report to the licensing authority any health condition likely to affect your driving.

RTA Sect 96
MV(DL)R No 20(1)(c) & Sch 4

Your eyesight **MUST** be up to the standard required for the driving test (see Rule 34 of the Code) at all times when you drive.

Drinking and driving
You **MUST NOT**:

RTA Sect 4

- drive under the influence of drink or drugs;

- drive with a breath alcohol level higher than 35 $\mu g/100$ ml (equivalent to a blood alcohol level of 80 mg/100 ml). **RTA** Sects 5 & 11(2)

5. ON THE ROAD
You **MUST** comply with:
- maximum speed limits (see page 53) or any special speed limit for your vehicle; **RTRA** Sects 81, 84, 86, 89 and Sch 6
- amber and red 'STOP' signals, traffic signs giving orders, double white lines and yellow road markings; **TSRGD** Nos 7, 23(1), 34(1) and Sch 2 **PPCRGD** No 16 **RTRA** Sects 1, 6 & 9
- the directions of a police officer or traffic warden controlling traffic. **RTA** Sect 35 **FTWO** No 3

You **MUST NOT**:
- drive dangerously; **RTA** Sect 2
- drive without due care and attention or without reasonable consideration for other road users; **RTA** Sect 3
- drive on a footway, footpath, bridle-way or cycle track at any time, or a bus or cycle lane during its hours of operation. **HA 1835** Sect 72 **RTRA** Sects 1, 6 & 9 **RTA** Sects 21 & 34 **R(S)A** Sect 129(5)

6. PEDESTRIAN CROSSINGS
Zebra and Pelican crossings
Pedestrians have precedence on the carriageway within the limits of a Zebra crossing, and on a Pelican crossing when the signal to cross is lit up. You **MUST** give way to pedestrians on a Zebra crossing or when an amber light is flashing on a Pelican crossing. **ZPCR** No 8 **PPCRGD** No 17

The carriageway on the approach to a Zebra or Pelican crossing is normally marked by zig-zag lines. In this area you **MUST NOT**:
- overtake the moving motor vehicle nearest the crossing; **ZPCR** No 10 **PPCRGD** No 19
- overtake the leading vehicle which has stopped to give way to a pedestrian.

School crossing patrols
You **MUST** stop when signalled to do so by a school crossing patrol exhibiting a 'STOP – CHILDREN' sign. **RTRA** Sect 28

7. DRIVING AT NIGHT OR IN REDUCED VISIBILITY
You **MUST**:
- ensure your front and rear side lights and rear registration plate lights are lit at night; **RVLR** No 24 **RV(R&L)R** No 19
- use headlights at night on all unlit roads and those where the street lights are more than 185 metres (600ft) apart; **RVLR** No 25
- use headlights when visibility is seriously reduced. **RVLR** No 25

You **MUST NOT**:
- use headlights in a way which would dazzle or discomfort other road users; **RVLR** No 27
- use front or rear fog lights unless visibility is seriously reduced; **RVLR** No 27
- sound your horn at night (11.30 pm to 7 am) in a built-up area. **CUR** No 99

8. WAITING AND PARKING

There are a number of places where the law specifically forbids you to let your vehicle stand. The most important of these are listed in Rules 138, 139 and 141 of the Code.

RTA Sect 22
CUR No 103

In addition there is a more general legal requirement that you **MUST NOT** park on the road in such a way that your vehicle or trailer is likely to cause danger to other road users or an unnecessary obstruction. Examples of places in which you are likely to be committing an offence are in Rule 140 of the Code.

9. PROVIDING INFORMATION TO THE POLICE

RTA Sect 163
RTA Sects 164 & 165

You **MUST** stop your vehicle when required to do so by a uniformed police officer, who may require you to produce documents including your driving licence, certificate of insurance and test certificate (MOT) for examination. If you are not carrying them with you, you may select a police station at which you can produce them within seven days.

10. ACCIDENTS

RTA Sect 170

If you are involved in an accident which causes damage or injury to any other person, or other vehicle, or any animal (horse, cattle, ass, mule, sheep, pig, goat or dog) not in your vehicle, or roadside property

You **MUST**:
- stop;
- give your own and the vehicle owner's name and address and the registration number of the vehicle to anyone having reasonable grounds for requiring them;
- if you do not give your name and address at the time of the accident, report the accident to the police as soon as reasonably practicable, and in any case within 24 hours.

If any other person is injured and you do not produce your insurance certificate at the time of the accident to the police or to anyone who with reasonable grounds has requested it, you **MUST** also:
- report the accident to the police as soon as possible, and in any case within 24 hours;
- produce your insurance certificate to the police either when reporting the accident or within seven days at any police station you select.

B TO MOTORCYCLISTS AND MOPED RIDERS

Most of the requirements of the law relating to drivers of motor vehicles also apply to you.

In addition you **MUST**:

MC(PH)R
CUR 57

RTA Sect 23
RTRA Sect 53

- wear an approved safety helmet on all journeys;
- ensure that your exhaust system and silencer are of an approved type;
- carry no more than one passenger on a motorcycle;
- not park in a parking meter zone except in a specially marked motorcycle park or (where not prohibited by a local order) at a meter.

Learners **MUST** comply with the requirements in Rule 37 of the Code.

Pillion passengers MUST:
- wear an approved type of safety helmet;
- sit astride the cycle on a proper seat securely fitted behind the driver's seat and with proper rests for the feet.

MC(PH)R
CUR No 102

C MOTORWAY DRIVING

Motorways **MUST NOT** be used by pedestrians, holders of provisional ordinary licences, pedal cycles, motorcycles under 50cc, invalid carriages not exceeding 254 kg unladen weight, certain slow-moving vehicles carrying oversized loads (except by special permission), agricultural vehicles and animals.

HA 1980 Sects
16, 17 & Sch 4
MT(E&W)R No 4
MT(E&W)(A)R
R(S)A Sects 7 & 8
MT(S)R No 10

You **MUST:**
- drive on the carriageways only;

- observe one-way driving on the carriageways;

- observe maximum speed limits (see page 53) or any special speed limit for your vehicle;
- observe flashing red signals when displayed over your lane or at the side of the carriageway;
- keep any animals in the vehicle or (in an emergency) under proper control on the verge.

MT(E&W)R No 5
MT(S)R No 4
MT(E&W)R No 6
MT(S)R No 5
RTRA Sects 17,
86 & Sch 6
RTA Sect 36
TSRGD No 34(4)
MT(E&W)R No 14
MT(S)R No 12

You **MUST NOT:**
- drive in reverse on the carriageway;

- stop on the carriageway; or on the hard shoulder (except in an emergency); or on the central reservation or verge.

MT(E&W)R No 8
MT(S)R No 7
MT(E&W)R
Nos 7(1), 9 & 10
MT(S)R Nos 6(1),
8 & 9

Motorways: right-hand lanes
You **MUST NOT** use the right-hand lane of a motorway with three or more lanes (except in prescribed circumstances) if you are driving
- any vehicle drawing a trailer;
- a goods vehicle with a maximum laden weight over 7.5 tonnes;
- a bus or coach longer than 12 metres.

MT(E&W)R No 12
MT(S)R No 10A

D TO PEDESTRIANS

You have precedence over other road users when you are on the carriageway within the limits of a Zebra crossing, and on a Pelican crossing when the signal to cross is lit. But you **MUST NOT** loiter on a pedestrian crossing.

ZPCR
PPCRGD

You **MUST NOT:**
- walk on motorways or their slip-roads;

- walk on the carriageway when directed not to do so by a police officer or traffic warden controlling traffic;
- hold on to or get on a moving motor vehicle or trailer.

RTRA Sect 17
MT(E&W)R No 15
RTA Sect 37

RTA Sects 25 & 26

E TO PEDAL CYCLISTS

You **MUST** obey the same rules as apply to drivers at pedestrian crossings and school crossing patrols (see A.6 on page 69).

(see A.6 on page 69)

In addition you **MUST**:

PCUR Nos 7–10
RVLR Nos 18, 23 & 24
RVLR No 24

RTA Sect 163

- ensure that your brakes are efficient;
- at night, ensure your front and rear lights are lit and that your cycle has an efficient red rear reflector;
- at night, if you are wheeling your cycle or are stationary without lights, keep as close as possible to the nearside edge of the road;
- stop when required to do so by a uniformed police officer or traffic warden.

You **MUST NOT**:

RTA Sect 28
RTA Sect 29

RTA Sect 30
HA 1835 Sect 72
R(S)A Sect 129(5)
RTA Sect 22

RTA Sect 24

RTA Sect 26

- ride dangerously;
- ride without due care and attention or without reasonable consideration for other road users;
- ride under the influence of drink or drugs;
- ride on a footway or footpath unless there is a right to do so;
- leave your cycle on any road in such a way that it is likely to cause danger to other road users, or where waiting is prohibited;
- carry a passenger on a bicycle not constructed or adapted to carry more than one person;
- hold on to a moving motor vehicle or trailer.

F TO HORSE RIDERS

You **MUST NOT** deliberately ride, lead or drive your horse:

HA 1835 Sect 72

R(S)A Sect 129(5)

H(PHYR)R

- on a footpath by the side of any road made or set apart for the use of pedestrians (England & Wales);
- on a footway, footpath or cycle track unless there is a right to do so (Scotland).

Children under 14 **MUST** wear a properly secured approved safety helmet.

PENALTIES

Parliament has set the maximum penalties for road traffic offences and within these maxima it is for the courts to decide what sentence to impose according to the circumstances. The maximum penalties for each offence are intended to reflect the seriousness of the offence.

The penalty table on page 74 indicates some of the main offences, and the associated penalties. (There are a wide range of other more specific offences which, for the sake of simplicity, are not shown here.)

The operation of the penalty points and disqualification system is described below.

PENALTY POINTS AND DISQUALIFICATIONS

1. For any offence which carries penalty points the courts have a discretionary power to order a period of disqualification. In the case of obligatory disqualification, the courts must disqualify for a minimum period of 12 months. For repeat offenders this may be longer. For example, a second drink-drive offence within 10 years will result in a minimum of three years' disqualification.

2. The penalty point system is intended to deter drivers from unsafe driving. The court must order penalty points to be endorsed on the licence according to the fixed number or within the range set by Parliament. The accumulation of penalty points acts as a warning to drivers that they risk disqualification if further offences are committed. Any driver who accumulates 12 or more points within a three-year period must be disqualified for a minimum period of six months and for a longer period if the driver has previously been disqualified.

OTHER CONSEQUENCES OF OFFENDING

3. In addition to the penalties a court may decide to impose, the cost of insurance is likely to rise considerably following conviction for a serious driving offence – in line with the increased risk of having an accident which insurance companies consider attaches to such drivers.

4. Drivers convicted of drinking and driving twice within 10 years, or once if they are over two and a half times the legal limit, or those who refuse to give a specimen, also have to satisfy the Driver and Vehicle Licensing Agency's Medical Branch that they do not have an alcohol problem and are otherwise fit to drive before their licence is returned at the end of their period of disqualification.

PENALTY TABLE

Offence	Maximum penalties			
	IMPRISONMENT	FINE	DISQUALIFICATION	PENALTY POINTS
*Causing death by dangerous driving	5 years	Unlimited	Obligatory – 2 years minimum	3–11 (if exceptionally not disqualified)
*Dangerous driving	2 years	Unlimited	Obligatory	3–11 (if exceptionally not disqualified)
Causing death by careless driving under the influence of drink or drugs	5 years	Unlimited	Obligatory – 2 years minimum	3–11 (if exceptionally not disqualified)
Careless and inconsiderate driving	–	£2,500	Discretionary	3–9
Driving while unfit through drink or drugs or with excess alcohol; or failing to provide a specimen for analysis	6 months	£5,000	Obligatory	3–11 (if exceptionally not disqualified)
Failing to stop after an accident or failing to report an accident	6 months	£5,000	Discretionary	5–10
Driving when disqualified	6 months (12 months in Scotland)	£5,000	Discretionary	6
Driving after refusal or revocation of licence on medical grounds	6 months	£5,000	Discretionary	3–6
Driving without insurance	–	£5,000	Discretionary	6–8
Driving otherwise than in accordance with a licence	–	£1,000	Discretionary	3–6
Speeding	–	£1,000 (£2,500 for motorway offences)	Discretionary	3–6 or 3 (fixed penalty)
Traffic light offences	–	£1,000	Discretionary	3
No MOT certificate	–	£1,000	–	–
Seat belt offences	–	£500	–	–
Dangerous cycling	–	£2,500	–	–
Careless cycling	–	£1,000	–	–
Failing to identify driver of a vehicle	–	£1,000	Discretionary	3

*Where a court disqualifies a person on conviction for one of these offences, it must order an extended retest – about twice as long as the ordinary driving test. The courts also have discretion to order a retest for any other offence which carries penalty points: an extended retest where disqualification is obligatory, and an ordinary test where disqualification is not obligatory

VEHICLE SECURITY

Over 2.5 million cars are broken into or stolen each year. That is one every 13 seconds.

A stolen car can mean having to walk home late at night. It can mean weeks of delay sorting out insurance, extra expense getting into work, loss of personal possessions, and losing your no-claims bonus.

So when you leave your vehicle always:
- Remove the ignition key and engage the steering lock.
- Lock the car, even if you only leave it for a few minutes.
- Close the windows **completely** – even the smallest gap is asking for trouble. But **never** leave children or pets in an unventilated car.
- Take all contents with you, or lock them in the boot. Remember, for all a thief knows a carrier bag may contain valuables. Never leave vehicle documents in the car.

For extra security fit an anti-theft device such as an alarm or immobiliser. If you are buying a new car it is a good idea to check the level of built-in security features. And it is well worthwhile having your registration number etched on all your car windows. This is a cheap and effective deterrent to professional thieves.

FIRST AID ON THE ROAD

For those with no first aid training.

DANGER – Deal with threatened danger or you and the casualties may be killed. FURTHER COLLISIONS and FIRE are the dangers in a road accident.

Action:
If possible warn other traffic. Switch off the engine. Impose a 'No Smoking' ban.

Obtaining further help:
Send a bystander to call an ambulance as soon as possible; state the exact location of the accident and the numbers of vehicles and casualties involved.

People remaining in vehicles:
Casualties remaining in vehicles should not be moved unless further danger is threatened.

If breathing has stopped:
Remove any obvious obstruction in the mouth. Keep the head tilted backwards as far as possible – breathing may begin and the colour may improve. If not, pinch the casualty's nostrils together and blow into the mouth until the chest rises; withdraw, then repeat regularly once every four seconds until the casualty can breathe unaided.

If unconscious and breathing:
Movement may further damage an injured back, so only move if in danger. If breathing becomes difficult or stops, treat as above.

If bleeding is present:
Apply firm hand pressure over the wound, preferably using some clean material, without pressing on any foreign body in the wound. Secure a pad with a bandage or length of cloth. Raise limb to lessen the bleeding, providing it is not broken.

Reassurance:
The casualty may be shocked but prompt treatment will minimise this; reassure confidently; avoid unnecessary movement; keep the casualty comfortable and prevent them getting cold; ensure they are not left alone.

Give the casualty NOTHING to drink.

Carry a first aid kit. Learn first aid – from the St John Ambulance Association and Brigade, St Andrew's Ambulance Association or the British Red Cross Society.

ISBN 0 11 550962 3

Prepared by the Department of Transport and
the Central Office of Information for HMSO

© Crown copyright 1993
New edition 1993
Third impression 1993
Printed in the UK for HMSO
Dd 296186C 7500 6/93

HMSO publications are available from:

HMSO Publications Centre
(Mail, fax and telephone orders only)
PO Box 276, London SW8 5DT
Telephone orders 071-873 9090
General enquiries 071-873 0011
(queuing system in operation for both numbers)
Fax orders 071-873 8200

HMSO Bookshops
49 High Holborn, London WC1V 6HB
071-873 0011 Fax 071-873 8200 (counter services only)
258 Broad Street, Birmingham B1 2HE
021-643 3740 Fax 021-643 6510
33 Wine Street, Bristol BS1 2BQ
0272 264306 Fax 0272 294515
9–21 Princess Street, Manchester M60 8AS
061-834 7201 Fax 061-833 0634
16 Arthur Street, Belfast BT1 4GD
0232 238451 Fax 0232 235401
71 Lothian Road, Edinburgh EH3 9AZ
031-228 4181 Fax 031-229 2734

HMSO's Accredited Agents
(see Yellow Pages)
and through good booksellers

Shortest Stopping Distances

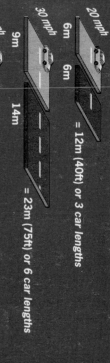

20 mph
6m
6m
= 12m (40ft) or 3 car lengths

30 mph
9m
14m
= 23m (75ft) or 6 car lengths

40 mph
12m
24m
= 36m (120ft) or 9 car lengths

50 mph
15m
38m
= 53m (175ft) or 13 car lengths

60 mph
18m
55m
= 73m (240ft) or 18 car lengths

70 mph
21m
75m
= 96m (315ft) or 24 car lengths

ISBN 0-11-550962-3

9 780115 509629